SPECIAL GRACE AND RESERVE GRACE

Question: What is the cause of poverty in the life of a Christian? How can a Christian have a reserve before God?

Answer: In Revelation 3 the Lord said, "You are...poor" (v. 17). These words were addressed by Him to the church in Laodicea. This poverty implies that nothing had been laid up in store. It implies not merely a momentary lack but a continuous lack.

A FUNDAMENTAL PROBLEM

Many brothers and sisters have a fundamental problem: They are maintained by the experience of special grace. This is a serious problem. They are dependent on temporary supplies of grace; they do not have the revelation which they saw "thirteen years ago." We have said before that God's work in our lives is wholly a work of grace. If He removed His grace from us, our lives would be an utter void. This is a fact which we need to recognize. Nevertheless, it is also a fact that God does not want to see His children devoid of any deposit of grace. He does not want them to be dependent on interventions of special grace in order to be kept in His will. It is not well-pleasing to Him if His children live from hand to mouth on special grace. He desires us to have a rich deposit of grace.

Many people have no such deposit. Consequently, the Lord told us to fast and pray. In Matthew 17:21 the Lord said that some demons could only be cast out by prayer and fasting. He told the disciples that they needed to have special prayer and fasting, without which they would not have the needed power. Christians whose loins are not girded, who are unrestrained, and whose spirits are wild have no choice but to live by special dispensations of grace. If we have just come to the Lord, it is understandable if we live by special grace; but if we are still dependent on such grace after we have believed in the Lord for a year or two, this indicates a state of poverty and sickness. This poverty is the result of living by special grace without having any extra or reserve grace.

What is wealth? Wealth is the reverse of poverty. Being spiritually wealthy means to have a reserve of grace before God and not to rely on special grace. Poverty is banished by the surplus of grace within.

PAUL HAVING RESERVE GRACE

The other day a few of us talked together about Paul's Epistles to the Corinthians. For my part I believe that the greatest revelation of life in the entire New Testament is in the Epistles to the Corinthians.

First and 2 Corinthians have their place; they are the only two Epistles that show us the man Paul. In his letter to the Romans he unfolds the matter of salvation in a profound way, and in his letter to the Ephesians he brings forth the deepest revelation. All of these things are from God. However, if we want to know Paul the person, we have to come to 1 and 2 Corinthians. Only these two books give us a clear understanding of Paul; they open up his very own person to us.

Many people cannot minister the word

of God apart from inspiration. If at any given time they have no fresh inspiration, their words stop. The source of their ministry of the word is their inspiration. It is a fact that we need inspiration if we are to have a ministry; there is nothing wrong about this. Please bear in mind the fact, however, that inspiration is not given to us in a stream of unbroken continuity. Even in the case of the first twelve apostles and in the case of such a person as Paul, inspiration was not continuous. In one instance he said, "I have no commandment of the Lord" (1 Cor. 7:25a). He did not have a word from the Lord; the Lord did not say anything. The Lord did not say it; he said it. In other words, he did not have revelation, spiritual inspiration, or any fresh word from the Lord.

But there is something amazing here. Paul said, "But I give my opinion as one who has been shown mercy by the Lord to be faithful [or honest]" (v. 25b). Paul was expressing his own judgment. What a terrific thing to do. Over the past nearly two thousand years, theologians have been afraid to touch these utterances of Paul,

WATCHMAN NEE

Special Grace and Reserve Grace

Living Stream Ministry
Anaheim, CA • www.lsm.org

ISBN 978-1-57593-864-6

Living Stream Ministry
2431 W. La Palma Ave., Anaheim, CA 92801
P. O. Box 2121, Anaheim, CA 92814 USA

Printed in India

18   19   20   21   22   /   7   6   5   4   3   2

but Paul knew what he was saying. When he was without immediate inspiration, he was still able to speak.

To speak without inspiration would be presumption on the part of others. Others have no word when they have no inspiration because they do not have extra reserves of grace. God only gives them enough grace for today. This kind of person does not have a word when they do not have immediate inspiration because they rely on special grace to meet the present need. Without special grace, they have nothing to say.

Here, however, we have a man who had a word without immediate inspiration. Paul's word was God's word. The Holy Spirit chose the word and put it into the Bible; we believe this was God's arrangement. Paul repeated several times that it was his word, not the Lord's. When he spoke, however, he indicated that the word did not seem to be his word, and he concluded with this remark: "I think that I also have the Spirit of God" (v. 40). It is very precious. He was unconsciously moved by the Holy Spirit. Some people are always ready to affirm that the Spirit is moving them. I am afraid that the very fact of their experience of immediate inspiration from the Holy Spirit betrays their shortage of a reserve. It is better to be moved by the Holy Spirit with no consciousness of the fact. Shallow people often doubt that they have not been moved by the Holy Spirit, while those with reserves doubt that they have indeed been moved. Is there some doubt that our word may be the Lord's word? Or are we "certain" that it is from the Lord?

We find a basic principle here. Paul had something other than immediate inspiration. He had a deposit apart from immediate inspiration. He had this deposit because for many years he had followed the Lord; he had been restricted; he had avoided sin and failure. For years he had learned to fear the Lord. Over these years, things were collecting within him. Although he did not have any immediate inspiration, he still had things to say. These were his reserve, or in other words, his riches.

No other Epistles unveil the person of Paul to us as his letters to the Corinthians. He tells us that he is only expressing his own judgment; he has no specific inspiration from the Lord. Yet we discover that what he uttered is actually a revelation to the church. Here is a man speaking his own words, and they are recorded in the Bible as the word of God. This touches the highest peak of the New Testament, where a man has been edified, carved, purified, and constituted by God to such an extent that his word becomes God's word. This is wealth. And this is an inward reserve which is the result of God's many years of work on Paul. Special grace cannot bring one to this peak.

THE NEED TO BE WEALTHY
WITH RESERVE GRACE

It is a great grief to me that I frequently meet brothers and sisters who are so dependent on special grace that between the periodic help these experiences bring, their words and state of mind lapse into that of a non-Christian. What a poverty-stricken state this reveals! Once this kind of person lacks an incoming supply, he is empty. I readily acknowledge that we all would be utterly destitute if God's grace were removed from us; but it is also true that something of God's grace can be constituted into our very being. God's reserve deposit in man is also a fact. Some people live from hand to mouth, spending whatever comes in to meet their expenses of the moment. They cannot withstand trials.

What are trials? Trials are times when it seems that God does not care for us, listen to us, or fellowship with us. Madame Guyon understood trials best. Spiritual trials are times when it seems that God has covered His face and shut His mouth, when it seems that He will not answer or make a sound, when it seems He is so quiet that there is no God in heaven at all. These times of trial immediately separate those with reserves from those with none.

A poor person lives by the joy of prayer and sustains his living through the freshness of the Lord's table. Whenever he does not have these, he fails for the week because he cannot go on, and he stumbles. Many people rely on special grace for their entire life and for all aspects of their living; they do not have reserves.

Some people, such as Madame Guyon, go through trials for months at a time. During the trials the entire world may appear so confusing that it seems as if there is no God. A person with inward reserves of grace will be manifested by such a time. He will pass the test. He has something inside that is sufficient. This something is called wealth. This is the wealth that the Lord spoke of to the church in Laodicea (Rev. 3:18a).

In summary, poverty is a lack of reserves; wealth is having reserves. We mean, of course, spiritual reserves.

HOW TO HAVE
A WEALTH OF RESERVES

Time Is an Essential Factor

How can we be inwardly wealthy with reserves? This is a question of fundamental importance. Permit me to say a very straight word to the younger brothers. No matter who you are, none of you are really wealthy. Perhaps you think you have become rich. But accumulating wealth requires time. Those who have spent time before God might have some riches. Those

who have not spent time without a doubt
are poor. It is impossible for young people
to be wealthy. Time is an important factor.
Formerly we were of the opinion that some
of the young people were ahead of the
older ones in basic spiritual matters. When
we recently touched some deeper matters
in Foochow, we discovered that many of the
finest young brothers were unable to grasp
the most practical matters. I appeal to you
young ones to check how much you have
accumulated in spiritual reserves. I am
afraid you only have the tiniest of reserves.
Do not be proud. Being proud is sheerest
folly. You must realize that a long course
still lies before you. You must be constituted with and established by the Holy
Spirit in this course day by day. Time is a
matter of primary importance. No one can
skip over this consideration.

Experiences
Are an Essential Factor

Second, we must go through various
experiences. Many people have spent much
time before God, but they have not passed
through many experiences before God. If

one wants to become rich, he must spend time before God, and he must pass through many experiences before God. The experiences one has to go through are the discipline of the Holy Spirit. Some people have been Christians for eight or ten years, but it seems as if the Holy Spirit is very lenient with them. It seems that He does not discipline them or even pay attention to them. It is as if the Holy Spirit does not want to concern Himself with their affairs. Other people, however, are taken in hand and not let off; they are severely disciplined by the Holy Spirit. It does not seem to matter what some people do, because the Holy Spirit does not speak to them through their situations or their consciences. Their situations do not give them much trouble, nor do their consciences. Even though these people have the benefit of the passage of much time, they do not learn much from God because they are not restricted, carved, hindered, and chastised enough. Therefore, they are not rich before God. For this reason, let us not be dismayed by the difficulties we face before God. Every one of these situations adds to our wealth.

The fewer problems we have, the less we will have in reserve, and the fewer words we will be able to share with others. No one can have a word without experience. Our wealth in the Word and our service to God's children are in proportion to the experiences we go through. Our supply comes through the lessons we have learned before God. This is not something that doctrines can give to us; nor is it something that commentaries on the Bible can give to us. It is something we learn when the Holy Spirit leads us in our daily walk.

Therefore, I hope that we will not be slack in our daily experience in learning to follow God. In all the disappointment and disillusionment we face, let us recognize the Lord's severe dealings with us. Let us bow before Him in gratitude and worship Him, acknowledging that His purpose in all these things is to enrich us and to lead us to abundance.

A certain brother thought that he was quite strong in faith until he fell ill. Then he began to learn the real meaning of faith. If we have never been poor, we do not know how to look to the Lord. If we have never been ill, we do not know faith. If we have never had problems, we do not know true worship. If we are without experiences and have not learned anything, we are poor. Anyone who tries to avoid difficulties is a poor person. Everyone who asks for easy circumstances is poor. If we want progress, we must ask for some situations to pass through. The more we want to learn, the more we must experience. Our hope, our faith, and our submission all come into these different situations to edify us and bring us through. If we have one more situation added outwardly, we will have one more item of spiritual wealth added inwardly. We must realize that every situation we encounter is for teaching us something, no matter how hard it is for our flesh or how much we dislike it. We must bow our head and say, "This is a chance, a once-in-a-lifetime chance, a hard to-come-by opportunity! Lord, I thank You!"

There are many people around us who are Christians, but some seem to be protected from trials. This kind of brother or sister has a very peaceful, quiet life, but we immediately sense that the faith, hope, and reliance of these saints are very small and poor.

Therefore, I hope you will listen to my frank words. When you encounter trials, you should lift up your head and praise the Lord, saying, "Lord, You are creating another opportunity within me for me to gain some riches. Everything is working together for good. You are going to produce something in me that others do not have so that I can supply the church." Brothers, do not be deceived into thinking that you will be able to preach by dint of much study. A man can deliver a message, but he does not necessarily have a rich spirit. A man can improve his preaching and increase the abundance of his words, but this does not make him wealthy in his spirit.

Being full of meaningful utterance and being full of the Spirit are two entirely different matters. God is not treating us wrongly when He gives us more trials and difficulties; He is actually treating us very well. He has selected us and has granted us favor by providing us this big opportunity. We must look for this. If we have the light, we should always consider one matter: How many experiences have we passed through before the Lord? Do we have any reserves? It does not matter how proud we are; our pride is worthless. If we have something inwardly, we have it; if we do not, we do not. The more we want to deceive others, the more they will know us. The prouder we are and the more we try to put on a good front, the more we will expose ourselves. Once we open our mouth, we expose ourselves. We should not presume that we can deceive others when our skin feels like Esau but our voice sounds like Jacob. The amount of our spiritual wealth is based on the amount of experiences we have passed through.

The Need for Finality

Third, finality is essential. It is not enough to go through many experiences. If we have spent the required amount of time and passed through the necessary experiences, we must ask if there has been a result. This can still be a problem. We must reach a place of finality. In carrying out a chemistry experiment in school, there is a principle: "Carry it to its finality." This means we must persist with the experiment until we get a result. Many times things are done but not thoroughly. If the work is not done thoroughly, it is useless. Everything must be thorough.

The Bible makes it abundantly plain that when God deals with a person, He does not let go easily; He does things thoroughly. It does not matter whether cattle are stolen, sheep and servants are burned, the house falls down, or the children die. It does not matter whether there are sores on the body. The lips and tongue must submit, and the mouth must be pressed to the dust (see Job 1:6—2:10; 42:1-6). Such a day must come. The Epistle of James uses the word *end* in 5:11, saying, "...his end from the Lord." Here we see that it is not a matter of the frequency of our trials but a matter of God reaching His end through the trials. Job's sons died. How many sons do we have that we can allow them to die? One person does not have that many sons to lose. This is a very serious matter. Job received a very heavy dealing, but he was still poor. We should not think that God can give us unlimited trials. There was a sister whose husband died, and she was a widow. However, she was very loose in spiritual matters. After she finished giving a testimony one day, I was very bothered inwardly. I spoke very frankly to her and said, "Your attitude is wrong. It is a serious matter that God took your husband away, but you have not learned the lesson! A person does not have that many husbands to lose." Many people want to go up to Kuling Mountain, but we should not think that Kuling is a nice place to go. Kuling is a place of heartless judgment. Your "cow and sheep" can be stolen, your "houses" can collapse, and your "sons" can die, but the matter still may not come to an end. Your entire body can be "covered with boils," but the matter still may not come to an end. This is the meaning of having no finality. A person must pass through many experiences, but there are only a limited number of situations he can go through. If a person does not learn the lessons from what he passes through, he cannot reach the end from the Lord. This means that the Lord will not attain His goal. Please remember that if the Lord does not gain anything, we will not have much reserve. If this is our case, we are just wasting the days, the dealings, the trials, and the discipline! This is a fearful matter. Many people go through dealings, but they become broken, useless vessels when they come out of them. This is like the potter's shop spoken of in Jeremiah 18:4. The floor is covered with vessels that did not turn out properly. Even though the vessels can claim that they have been put into the fire, they remain broken on the floor.

Therefore, our hope is not only that we would spend sufficient time before the Lord and pass through enough experiences, but also that we would become vessels unto glory after we pass through these experiences.

Job did not just pass through experiences. One day God saw that a point of finality had come. There was a new constitution in him; he had changed. This is a matter of fundamental importance. It is not a matter of receiving more life, but a matter of constituting the human life with the divine life.

I will make a statement that I fear is

often misunderstood by people: The old man cannot be changed. It is a fact that God has crucified the old man, and it is also a fact that God has put a new life within us. If God took this life away, the old man would still be the old man. However, the Bible also says that man can be changed and that the mind can be renewed and transformed (Rom. 12:2). Please remember that it is not merely the new life within us that makes us different from others; we become different from others by the working of this new life within us. When we live with someone for a long time, we begin to resemble that person. When we live together with God for a long time, it is really strange if we do not change in the slightest. Since the Holy Spirit lives in us, there must be something that we have learned of Him that makes us like Him. This is renewing and transformation.

Therefore, we hope to learn our lessons, and we hope to arrive at a finality. Hopefully, the time we spend before God and the lessons we have learned before Him will have an end. The Lord put His Spirit inside us to enable us to learn the lessons and reach an end. Only then will the Lord be able to use us to supply others. We cannot obtain this from reading or from listening to Paul; it only comes from learning Christ (Eph. 4:20). We do not do things merely because the Bible says so. We do them because we have learned them for ourselves. We must have this quality before we can serve God and before our words can supply others.

Light Is Also Necessary

The last thing needed is light. A person who is rich is one who receives much light. We must not just learn the lessons; the Lord must also enlighten us in spirit so that we see what we are learning. We do not merely know that something has happened. What has happened must be molded into a teaching in us. This is the only way we will be able to turn our experience into words to supply others. The situation does not just happen to us. We are able to take what we have learned and supply it to others. When the light comes, we can speak, and our words will supply others.

God often deals with us, but we do not know it. Sometimes, however, we know. This knowing makes the dealing more effective in reaching its end. We can believe and obey because of the enlightenment. Therefore, we can quicken the end of the dealing. Fruit is brought forth, and this fruit is ripened. This is man's end before God. This kind of enlightenment is the eyesalve spoken of in Revelation 3:18. It enables one to see and to shine.

ENLIGHTENMENT BEING DIFFERENT
FROM INSPIRATION

Question: Is the enlightenment which you speak of different from inspiration?

Answer: Yes, it is different. This light comes through revelation; it is an inward light. The basic problem with the inward being is the matter of obedience.

CONCERNING THE DISCIPLINE
OF THE HOLY SPIRIT

Question: When a situation comes to us, we should submit as quickly as possible, but does this kind of swift submission depend on swiftly acknowledging that this situation is from the Lord?

Answer: Yes, that is true, but it is important for us to understand the meaning of the discipline of the Holy Spirit.

The discipline of the Holy Spirit means that when the Holy Spirit is operating in our outward circumstances to bring us to a particular goal, He is also making an inward demand on us. This operation is called the discipline of the Holy Spirit. If we do not obey, it will not serve His purpose immediately. But even if we do not submit, He will bring us to the point of obedience. A day will definitely come when He will make us submissive. The discipline of the Holy Spirit often brings about our submission. This is not to say that we have the will to submit in ourselves, but we are brought to the point where we obey spontaneously. Brothers and sisters who have believed in the Lord for many years can look back on their lives and count many times when the Lord spoke to them and they obeyed. The Lord spoke again, and they obeyed again. We can all say this. If we look back and think, we can identify many times when the Lord spoke and we had no intention to obey. Yet, in the end we obeyed. This is the result of the discipline of the Holy Spirit. Sometimes we actually set our mind on disobeying, yet mysteriously, after two or three years of confusion, our resistance fades away, and the disobedience is no longer there. This is the result of the discipline of the Holy Spirit. When we submit by ourselves, the job is done soon. But thank God, even when we have no heart to submit, and there is no faith, we can still be brought to the point of submission. This is a result of the discipline of the Holy Spirit. I often consider the discipline of the Holy Spirit to be a measure whereby He fills up our own lack of submission.

There are two aspects of the discipline of the Holy Spirit. The first is to cause us to submit. God arranges our environment and calls us to submission. The second is the discipline of the Holy Spirit in taking over our submission. We do not have any intention of submitting, but the Holy Spirit works on us to the extent that we submit nevertheless.

There was a brother who loved money very much. The Holy Spirit disciplined him many times, but he still loved money. During the past three or four years, many things came across his way which made him very angry. Today, however, unconsciously he no longer loves money. He has asked, "Must my love for money be given up in a spirit of obedience? What if I give it up in a spirit of disobedience?" I have answered that as long as he has given up his love for money, it is all right. Many times we want to submit quickly, and we ask God to give us grace that we might submit. This is very good. This will cause us to go through less chastisement; it can save us some dealings. We can reach the other side more quickly. But even if we are not that cooperative, He will bring us through according to His good timing as long as we give Him the time. This is the discipline of the Holy Spirit. Therefore, the inward working of the Holy Spirit is precious, and the outward working of the Holy Spirit through our environment is also very precious.

Question: How can we obey more quickly?

Answer: Sometimes God's Holy Spirit

works in us inwardly through His operation; sometimes He works on us through the passage of time. When the Holy Spirit of God moves within us, obedience is instant. But God does not only work through His Holy Spirit within men; He also works in men through the outward discipline of the Holy Spirit. This is not immediate. It is a day-by-day process. He continues this work until one day we are both willing and changed. This takes time however. When we ask God to give us submission, there are two kinds of answers to this prayer: inward operation, which is instant, and outward environment, which takes time. Thus, we are able to submit either through enlightenment or through discipline.

The day will come when the church will reach full maturity as depicted in Ephesians 4. Then the church will be without spot or wrinkle or any such things, as mentioned in Ephesians 5. Here are two sides to the work: John wept when he saw that no one was worthy to open the scroll (Rev. 5:4). I do not think that we are like John, but readers of the Bible become very worried about Ephesians 4 and 5. It seems

as if it is easier to consider stars like figs
and hailstones that weigh a talent falling
to the earth than it is to think of the
church maturing and arriving at the full
stature of Christ, no longer having spots
or wrinkles or any such things. It worries
them to think that the church has to be so
holy that it becomes absolutely irreproachable, being able to present itself for open
scrutiny and not be found with any flaw or
criticism. We see, however, that the Holy
Spirit not only works inwardly but also
disciplines outwardly to bring us to the
point of being irreproachable. How real is
the discipline of the Holy Spirit! We strug-
gle to deal with many things, but many
things are dealt with unconsciously. Our
Lord has arranged all kinds of things for
us; He has planned our future. This is truly
the Christian gospel! It is marvelous to
realize that Christians have the discipline
of the Holy Spirit.